Travelling
with the
Saints

First impression: 2013
© Copyright remains with the
individual contributors & Y Lolfa Cyf., 2013

Cover design: Y Lolfa

ISBN: 978 1 84771 702 3

Published and printed in Wales
on paper from sustainable forests by
Y Lolfa Cyf., Talybont, Ceredigion SY24 5HE
website www.ylolfa.com
e-mail ylolfa@ylolfa.com
tel 01970 832 304
fax 01970 832 782

Travelling
with the
Saints

edited by Peter Walker

Peter Walker is an Anglican priest in the diocese of St Asaph. As part of the 'H'mm Foundation', he has been adopted as the Church in Wales poet for 2013/2014.

The present collection has been put together as part of the St Asaph 'Year of Pilgrimage', and it is hoped that it will prove to be a source of spiritual encouragement to all those who seek to make their own pilgrimage, however they interpret that word!

The poet-contributors come from across the diocese – from Bistre to Bala – from Prestatyn to Pennant Melangell – from Llanddulas to Llandegla – and their work is as varied as their locations.

May you find something here to light a spark in your own heart.

Contributors

With grateful acknowledgement to all those who contributed poems:

Doreen Atkinson
Sally Baird
Glenda Beagan
Maureen Coppack
Frances Culver
Emyr Davies
Gwyneth Davies
Lynne Davis
Linda Mary Edwards
David Eglington
Denise Eglington
Alyson Evans
Phyl Evans
Jean Fuller
Manon Ceridwen James
Helen Jenkin Jones
Daphne Jones

Isobel Jones
Sue Last
Sylvia Mandeville
E. Gwynn Matthews
Gwyn Parry
John Poolman
Caren Price
Janet Robinson
Llewelyn Rogers
Sally Rogers
Andrew Sumner
Patricia Sumner
Marjorie Taylor
Derek Thorp
Peter Walker
Margaret Williams

May you continue to grow on your journey and draw others into the excitement of the voyage!

Peter Walker
Editor

Introduction

It is a truism of our times that while people are happy
to describe themselves as 'spiritual' they shun the word
'religious'.

And one way in which today's spirituality is manifested
is in the popularity of the idea of 'pilgrimage' – a journey of
discovery and self-discovery that seeks to connect with the
Ground of Being/God in a personal and revelatory way. It is
through pilgrimage that religion and spirituality are linked
in a direct and symbiotic way, whether the ancient pilgrim
route to Santiago de Compostella, or along the new North
Wales Pilgrim's Way, or a more individual quest to a holy site
or even an 'inner pilgrimage' within oneself.

As a way of linking the life of the Diocese of St Asaph
with this emerging spirituality, it was decided to undertake a
diocesan initiative by holding 'A Year of Pilgrimage' running
from St Asaph's Day 2013 (5 May) to St Asaph's Day in
2014. It was suggested that I might like to contribute some
poems on the theme of pilgrimage, but it seemed too good
an idea not to open it up to the people in the diocese, and I
am grateful for their positive response. The task was to offer
a poem which resonated with the year of pilgrimage in some
way, whether referring to an actual pilgrimage or to one of
the holy sites around the diocese of which there are many.

We trust that readers will find something to inform their own voyage of discovery, maybe to feel inspired to express their own experiences in a literary form or, indeed, to make a journey of their own to one of the places described here.

Those who gather Sunday by Sunday, week by week, in our churches would, I guess, be happy to describe themselves as both 'religious' and 'spiritual'. God's pilgrim people on a voyage of discovery, seeking to discover who they are, how God calls them, and using the metaphor of 'journey' to travel into both the secrets of their own soul and into an experience of the life and purpose of Jesus Christ. They do this through worship, study, sharing, community, prayer and fellowship, a personal quest informed and affirmed by others on that same voyage and very much in the tradition of the Celtic saints in whose path the Church in Wales is rooted and from which it draws its spirituality, grounded as it is in that quest to see God's face in all aspects of His world and His children.

And let no-one forget that before the followers of Jesus were known as Christians they were simply People of the Way!

PETER WALKER

Prologue

I take the name of psalm-bringer

from monks' house to saints' rest
ascending to the holy places
across the storms of mountains
& the high hill seas

with awe before the void
or the phenomenology of our emotions
anger at my own complicity in the world's woes
shame at my secret lives
joy in the simplicity of little things
in the woodwind cuckoo and the blackbird flute
the intermingling emulsion of our genes

& so we make a pilgrimage of words
into the inner workings of our vocabulary
where we stand in silence
before the dyslexic letters of our perception
seeking to make sense with the grammar of our morality
& thus construct a narrative of grace
for our journey's end

yet however far we travel we are drawn into ourselves
to echoes, souls, to apophasis, darkness, light

such is the emptiness we seek
to find it filled with possibility

PETER WALKER

Sonnet

Why do we long to go on pilgrimage?
What draws our hearts? To seek a greater truth?
A yearning for our distant heritage?
Beguiled by Chaucer's 'Aprill shoures soote'?
Or challenged by the road to Compostella,
To earn the right the scallop shells to wear?
Or weighted down by sins fast rush to hell
We drag up steep Croagh Patrick's Mount, feet bare?
John Bunyan urged us never to relent
Our first avowed intent to be a pilgrim.
And psalmist David grasped the truth, heav'n sent,
Which gripped his soul and filled him to the brim:
True pilgrimage, through years of Godly orderings
Alone can change life's arid wilderness to springs.

SYLVIA MANDEVILLE

The Pilgrimage of Life

WITH OUR FIRST BREATH WE BEGIN THE
PILGRIMAGE OF LIFE
WE LEARN GOD'S LOVE FROM WORDS FROM
ABOVE
WITH HIM WE TAKE EACH STEP ALONG THE
WAY
AS WE GROW AND GROW DAY BY DAY
LIFE THROWS AT US ALL KINDS OF HIGHS AND
LOWS
BUT OUR STRENGTH COMES FROM OUR TRUST
IN THE LORD
WE TAKE THE LONG JOURNEY FROM START TO
FINISH
AND AT THE END OF OUR DAYS THE
PILGRIMAGE COMES TO AN END
WHEN WE ARE AT LONG LAST BACK IN THE
ARMS OF THE LORD

DOREEN ATKINSON

Pilgrimage (Walking with strangers)

Walking with strangers
as friends,
to new stones

away, to the edge
or towards the centre,
Enlli, Rome.

Searching for
a memory,
in the present tense.

Looking for the well
we long for
in the wrong place.

God is always here
this time,
this space.

Manon Ceridwen James

Pilgrimage (We are walking)

WE ARE WALKING ON A
PILGRIMAGE
WE ARE WALKING ON A
PILGRIMAGE
WE ARE WALKING ON A
PILGRIMAGE

WHEN WE GET THERE
WE PRAY TO GOD
WHEN WE GET THERE
WE PRAY TO GOD
WHEN WE GET THERE
WE PRAY TO GOD

WE ALL SING
WE ALL SING
WE ALL SING

WE ARE WALKING ON A
PILGRIMAGE
WE ARE WALKING ON A
PILGRIMAGE
WE ARE WALKING ON A
PILGRIMAGE

JEAN FULLER

Our Christian Pilgrimage

'I cannot be an angel, or a saint.'
'True,' said he, 'but a pilgrim you may be.'
'I have no courage. My Faith is too faint.'
'Just take the first step, trustfully,' said he.

On my pilgrimage now, slowly, I tread,
Taking just one step, one hour, one day,
Knowing that challenges may be ahead,
Growing in Faith and remembering to pray.

Some hours I walk with others. We share pain.
Often we stumble and often we fail.
Yet, seeing a rainbow after the rain,
We believe that Love will always prevail.

Needing forgiveness, we learn to forgive,
Pausing to care for sisters and brothers,
As we learn from Christ the Way we should live:
Loving and sharing and serving others.

MARGARET WILLIAMS

The 2013 Pilgrims of St Asaph

Pilgrims from across St Asaph, are
Wondering what is going to happen
As we start our pilgrimage, our
Journey to many a special place.

Sharing tales along the way,
Listening to what others say
Each step we take has a meaning
Sometimes though it isn't easy.

We don't often know the way ahead
We try to follow as we are led
Lots of steps out there to tread,
For all our needs to be spiritually fed.

There are lots of other pilgrims
All over our world today, so
We join with them in our Pilgrim Year
And pray for them each day.

GWYNETH DAVIES

Pilgrimage (The infant...)

The infant, all unknowing and unknown,
Driven from the warm, dark hollow of the womb
By some force not its own, slips, loudly wailing,
Helpless, into light.

The child, all-trusting, free of care, unstained,
Weaves its own way through childhood's tortuous maze;
Days, months and years appear to last forever,
And the road leads on.

Young men and women take their place, and stumble
Through the humdrum world of work, no work, and play;
They search out paths through life's rough, stony places,
And must find the way.

The older folk, with more time now to stare,
Remembering generations lost from sight,
Look back at those who follow on the road,
And draw near their goal.

The soul, at last, all-knowing and all-known,
Deaf to the turmoil of the busy world,
Steals softly from the confines of its shell,
Finding timeless Light.

Frances Culver

The Pilgrimage

I walked along the path on a wet and gloomy morn
My spirits high to where I was heading
I reached the road so journeyed on
Deep in thought and prayers for peace to come

I reached my destination, my journey's end
The sun shone bright, with dark clouds gone
My spirits high with time to spend
In prayer and love to carry on

A new place, new friends, all quiet together
Help me, Lord, at the beginning and the ending
To find the strength and courage to stay
Closer to you, dear Lord, each and every day

MARJORIE TAYLOR

Pilgrimage (If I could turn back time...)

If I could turn back time and have a key,
I would visit the places most important to me;
Where I learned in the Bible of my Saviour's love,
How He became the path to Heaven above.

The first is my Sunday school, long since gone,
Where I learned of my Saviour, that He was the One
Who would willingly love me and be my guide;
If I would just trust Him, He'd stay by my side.

The second's my school, those memorable years
Where I heard of His love, that He shed blood-filled tears
And died on His cross for the sins I would do,
So I could believe that He loved me too.

The third is a guest house where Christians met
For a weekend retreat about sin and regret,
"If you have faith like a small mustard seed
It will grow into all the assurance you need."

My pilgrimage is the path I now walk
With Jesus, just listening and hearing Him talk
Of the place I will dwell when the time is right,
And I will be resting in Heaven's delight.

DENISE EGLINGTON

Michaelmas Day in Llanfihangel

See Michael, we have come to pray in your Church
On this feast of all the holy angels
Bless to us the harvest of crop and beast
Protect our byres
      Where grain and fleece are stored
Keep in safety
      Us winter travellers
Who must soon face night's darkness
And the storms scourgings
Guide us through
      These days when the year is dying
Out into the light
      Which lies beyond the sunset
Lead us on to that time
      When lamb and daffodil
Dance out their victory.

JOHN POOLMAN

Friends Together

Friends and family all together,
Doesn't matter what the weather.
Twenty-five people, what a lot
All gathering at a meeting spot.

God created heaven and earth,
We believe, for what it's worth,
All God's creatures everywhere
If only we made time to stare.

Walking down a lane, finding a brook
Stopping and taking time to look.
Dogs and children having a splash
Everyone else having a laugh.
We're nearly at our journey's end
But most of all, we made friends.

Caren Price

Reflections on Christmas Eve

It is a still, starry night.
Jack Frost unfurls his fingers
Claiming everything within his path.
The ancient church glistens in the moonlight on the eve of
　　Christmas.
Inside, preparations for celebration of our Saviour's birth.
Candle flames dance in the darkness,
Holly and ivy adorn the lintels,
The ancient walls tremble in anticipation.
The bell rings out a call to celebrate.
Then, the click of the church gate.
The crunch of feet on frosty ground – repeat of Pilgrims
　　past.
Mumbled voices from beneath woollen scarves wrapped
　　tightly to keep out the chill.
Then inside, voices swell in carol song.
'Tis such a glorious sound.
God's presence is felt.
His presence is here.
Still within these ancient walls and beyond, and within each
　　one of us,
God is working His purpose out.
With the celebration of our Saviour's birth, Be Still…
The spirit of Christmas lives on in our sad, mad world.

Lynne Davis

Plygain

*(The journey on Christmas morning to Hen Gapel John
Hughes, Pontrobert)*

The lane led off from the light into a narrow dark where the
leaves of summer are composted, carpeting the tarmac until
track and verge merge, disconcerting were it not for the fury
of a brook pressing past, urgent in the ear. Instinct draws me
on, foot-feeling and meeting a low glow from above, where
the moon and clouds should have been. It was fragmented
through a tracery of twigs and there were voices over the
water's rush.

There is a "clicied" on the door, I know, and pressing
it opens candles-glow that becomes a wrap of warmth as
people move like clothed shadows, speaking, greeting, quiet
under John Hughes' pulpit, silent-saved into the pause where
the Infant is calling, pointing. The low light is pressed to
the walls as the people bend into chairs and benches. The
prayers are said, a hymn sung and the waited words are
heard – "Mae'r Plygain yn agored" – opening a silence,
poised, understood, that reaches its height in the gathering
of a group. The fork strikes a hum and harmony and the
story is begun, to the tight interweaving of voices singing,
spine-tingling, the understanding of their forefathers' writing
faith on farm-house kitchen tables. Scholarship of the Spirit
spills and stains the present with marks that last beyond the
reach of modern bleach, taking the heart to meet the Infant,
calling, pointing. Silence is left to reign again, waiting the
same quiet crescendo, now, into a solo story drawn from a

root reaching our beginnings and the wound carried across time, its weeping wrapped with love until this final healing, held by the Infant, calling, pointing. "Iechydwriaeth" – "Gorfoleddwn" colour each singing-telling. Rapped in the repeated truth rolling, we subside into a final silence – y Gras – and leave again into the dark carried on the power of the water at our side and feeling the new gathering of light from the Infant, calling, pointing.

LLEWELYN ROGERS

Soned i Nia Rhosier

(Composed by local poet, Emyr Davies, Llangadfan in recognition of Nia's vision in establishing and running the Centre for Christian Unity & Renewal in Hen Gapel John Hughes, Pontrobert, which was restored after twelve years of fundraising through a national appeal in 1995, and which is now featured in the Living Stones Pilgrim trail.)

Ailgynnaist ym Mhontrobert yr hen dân
Fu gynt yn llosgi, cyn troi'n lludw llwyd,
Lle bu dyheu am 'Anfon Ysbryd Glân'
Ac awdur *Pren Planedig*, yn ei nwyd.
Cartre'r emynydd craff ac ysgolhaig,
A fu'n pregethu'r gair o lan i lan.
A'r fan cofnodai Ruth, ei ddiwyd wraig,
Eiriau angerddol y 'Fendigaid Ann',
Bu John, Pendugwm yma'n plygu glin
Cyn mentro i Tahiti ar ei daith
I brofi bywyd newydd, caled, blin
Wrth hybu neges Crist fel rhan o'i waith.
Fe sylwaist di ar werth y 'Gweithdy Saer'
A'i droi yn deml, cartref gweddi daer.

EMYR AP ERDDAN

A Visit to St Asaph's Cathedral

Knees have knelt here for centuries
On these ancient flagstones:
Carboniferous limestone
From the Mesozoic years,
Marked with comma-shaped fossils,
The Masoretic text of time.

Yet, before even the foundations were laid,
Before even the layering of these rocks,
Is the Ancient of Days
Claiming us in Him
To kneel here – in this cool hush,
The Living Life reclaiming us –
As He proclaimed those worshippers
Who came here all those years ago,
And as He claims now
Those who are yet unborn
To kneel here and bow.

Sylvia Mandeville

Homeward Bound

As I write these lines on my laptop,
Music is playing quietly in the background.
My thoughts reflect on DVDs I watched on previous
    evenings.
A Venetian made a voyage following a Mediterranean trade
    route
sailed by his ancestors 500 years earlier.
His voyage in a 100-year-old sailing ship took him to
    interesting places,
beautiful churches, and centres of pilgrimage visited by
    thousands of people.

Home – to where my Comforter waits for me
Home – to Him who does all things well
Home – to He who lived and died for me
Home – to the One my heart longs to see
Why does the apparent mediocrity of my pilgrimage give
    Him such delight?

I reflect on my life being a pilgrimage not to a place,
but to a person of unspeakable beauty and infinite glory.
Walking – in a different place yet in His footsteps
Walking – in a different culture yet in His Way
Walking – in a different time yet in His presence
Not seeing clearly, yet always
Walking – towards Him who is the way, the truth, and the
    life.

A pilgrimage in which the way we make the journey
is as significant as the destination.
Learning that He who walked with fishermen from Galilee,
Is comfortable sitting next to me whose tools are the internet,
computer & MP3.

David Eglington

Pilgrimage (Oh to be a pilgrim)

"Oh, to be a pilgrim"
My Father said to me;
Along the journey we go
In fellowship with Thee.

Take in the spirit of the land
On our pilgrim's way,
Wells and shrines, all at hand
Around and about Conway.

People in motion, gathered
In friendship we glow;
To find the emotion, forward
And further we will go.

Those distant childhood days
When adventure was such joy,
We travel on once more
Embracing the pilgrim's way.

PHYL EVANS

Greenman's Road

Six months ago he had walked the same road
Leading home, across the mountain
That day, the ground was frozen, and
   the path slippery.
Today the sun was burning down
On the lane high with summer,
High as the banks which lined it on either side.
A green road, before the tarmac came
Wales and Cornwall, both are lands of promise
With little to choose between them
Blindfold the traveller,
   and who would know the difference.

John Poolman

Holywell to Bardsey Island
August 2011

Sacred places
Peaceful places.
Walking on carpets of flowers.
Bells ringing to welcome us.
Shelter from the wind and rain.
Sanctuary.

These are the thoughts from our Pilgrimage.

Yet in the English cities there was rioting
Oh that we could give those young people the opportunity
  of experiencing the freedom of the Pilgrimage.

To feel the sun, the wind and the rain.

To walk alongside each other, sharing the experience.
Walking in the footsteps of those ancients who had been
  before us.

We were twenty-first-century Pilgrims, a million miles from
the riots and war zones, cocooned by the tranquillity of
the countryside, the fellowship of our companions, and the
Spiritual refreshment found in those Holy Places.

SUE LAST

Treffynnon (Holywell)

My three-year-old son and I
are caught unawares
by this dark tower of water.

I hold him on the wall edge
and I hold him tight.
We both feel the need to dive

to clean ourselves in the pulse,
the bubble of this
1,000-year-old spring.

Black gothic stone needles
above our heads.
Names of the healed

scratched initials – 1651.
My son says,
Amser maith yn ôl.

But before, before the rosary's drone,
before pigeons ever landed
on this dark stone

before the Church
made this place their own,
before the first pilgrim.

Long before the first factories,
the failed industrial estate
and the dirt of a modern road.

Gwenfrewi lost her head
to Caradog's angry sword.
Her head fell

to be cradled
by strong clean water,
her blood, coloured the river copper.

GWYN PARRY

The Pilgrimage (St Michael & All Angels Parish Church, Trelawnyd)

The bell tolls as I look at the clock,
Calling the faithful to prayer.
How many faithful are there now?
Answ'ring the call seems so rare.

Out of the house I slowly go,
Along the road, down the slope.
St Michael's Church appears again,
A beacon of light and hope.

Through the Lyche Gate arch I pass,
Along the "Old" graveyard––
Among those people who helped me on
The Headmistress who worked so hard.

The Churchyard is so peaceful here,
Clumps of snowdrops breaking through,
All God's creation to us is shown,
His love just grew and grew.

The grass grows greener there,
The birds sing loudly too,
Down to the "New" churchyard I go,
Remembering friends I once knew.

As I retrace my steps I see
The Preaching Cross standing so tall.

It stood here long before the Church
Was built and given to all.

The bell tolls louder now and so
Into the porch I quickly walk
Through the old door with its quaint old key
If only it could talk!

I take a seat and bow in prayer,
Then look at the window in front of me
Where Jesus my Saviour is dying––
Dying for all on the Tree.

This is my pilgrimage, you see,
My village Church leads me to Thee.

DAPHNE JONES

St Tecla's Well

Modestly the well hides amongst trees,
Across fields, close to the river.
A visiting pilgrim now sees
Its stone lined-basin and clear water
Sometimes full of leaves.

Old stone heads were found nearby,
A fallen stile might be a cross.
Once, perhaps, was there a canopy,
Steps for bathers,
A path, a gateway?

A complex ritual was invented:
A night in church, head on the Bible,
The Lord's Prayer recited
Anticlockwise, round and back,
In hopes epilepsy might be conquered.

A cockerel pricked and pins in the well,
Maybe roast dinner for the Rector,
Superstitions and magic spells
Now near forgotten.
Yet still this quiet place holds its mystery.

JANET ROBINSON

Holy Well

walled by stone
from deep below
in linen chalk
limestone-wrapped

this dribble

ooze of pus on mountain face
lapped by furry tongue of moss
taste of rusty nail & blood
chalybeate & corked bordeaux
bitter hyssop, spittle, death

leaks

until the chalice overflows
& builds
Slow... slow... slow...
to cataract of pigeon wing
that dins my ear
with multiplicity of language babble
tumbling phoneme foam
mandarin, xhosa, essex drawl
scally, brummy, hint of cappadocia

& flows

murky... mingled... messy...
into the grateful salty tears
of this waiting presence

Peter Walker
(from *Penmon Point*, 2011)

Pennant Melangell

We tread –
in the well-worn footsteps
of saints and strangers.

The blur of hedgerows, catches the eye
as time – slips – beneath our feet.

The ebb and flow of conversation
broken only
by silence
and the bleating of sheep.

The sun rises,
Layers are shed,
Secrets laid bare.

WE STOP
to nurse blistered heels and rest aching limbs.

Then onwards,
as the mist lifts its skirts
to protect its new found friend.

SALLY BAIRD

Melangell

On a deserted day,
abandoned to shade,
we snaked and twined
on ways steep-climbing.
Followed a balcony lane
clinging to mountain
over plunging valley,
where sky, heavy as mercury
and littering snow, decried
our resolve, our journey.
Descending into green,
the road ribboned
into hushed stillness
in the dish of the hills.
And, tentative as hares
creeping under a maiden's hem,
we entered the church. In silence,
made our own path to peace
and the One who led Melangell
to offer herself.

Patricia Sumner

With Saint Melangell in Cwm Pennant
(In the footsteps of Elijah) (1. Kings 19)

Base earth and bracken
draws me into her valley
fluent in slate scales,
moss, ewes, rock and roots;
tailings of the industry and the ice
under a sky leaching moods
and crescendos, leaving
stillness for stillness, long
as the threads of lichen.

I am tossed by my straits,
striated, complaining my
loneliness in spite of the voice;
resenting his questions that
brought me – answering
isolation.

Reluctant to wait, to watch,
I resist and yearn, both,
am reduced in the feel of fears
resonating so loud I cannot
hear a melting in the ice.

Here, the singular friend comes
calling again his questions
and allowing me not to
understand what I do.
"Why am I here"?
"I, alone":
hounded, cloaked in the skirts
of this valley – inclined towards
the Whisper.

LLEWELYN ROGERS

Pennant Melangell

An unlikely turn
off a B road
on to a winding, narrow track with blind bends.
You have to go slowly.
Sheep
who have always been there
go on chewing,
hardly noticing
a new pilgrim passing.
The track seems to follow a stream but leads nowhere,
ending in the dirt of a farmyard.
Lost and dependent now, I have to ask directions.
The farmer obliges: he knows the way.
In disbelief, I continue:
can this strange and unmarked way
lead anywhere?
More fields, the odd house, and then, oh, then...
Nestled against a hillside, a backdrop of breathtaking beauty,
an ancient stone church,
the place of encounter.
The thud of silence as I enter
'to kneel where prayer has been valid'.
I feast on the abundance of God's house.
I drink from the river of God's delights.
I have come home.

LINDA MARY EDWARDS

Pererindod

Tramwyo,
troedio,
teithio.
Cyd-deithio gyda ffrind i
chwilio amdano.
i ddyfnhau profiad,
i rannu gweddi,
i ddod o hyd i esmwythder er mwyn derbyn sefyllfa.
I deimlo yn well.
I allu byw.

Prancio yr ŵyn a sisial y dŵr wrth iddo redeg dros y cerrig.
Bref y ddafad, a rhu hirbell y tractor nad oedd yn y golwg.
Tai, bythynnod twt ac ambell un angen ei atgyweirio.
Iorwg yn nadreddu dros foncyffion yn gorwedd,
yn mygu y mwswgl,
y rhisgyl, y goeden, y bywyd.
Blagur y llwyni ar bob ochr yn uwch na'n pennau
yn amddiffynfa rhag y gwynt.
Trydar adar, a thapio Cnocell y Coed.
Cam wrth gam,
Gair am air.
Saib,
Tawelwch,
Sgwrsio a rhannu,
Dagrau glaw.
Diferynion crio.
Chwerthin.

Ffrind.

Ac yna ar y dde roedd yr Eglwys.
Coed ywen o'i chwmpas.
Yn fach, yn ddiaddurn
ac eto yn hardd.
Wedi herio pob tywydd.
Wedi cynnal teuluoedd ers blynyddoedd.
Bedyddio, priodi a chladdu
Patrwm y rhod, patrwm y bywyd Eglwysig,
Patrwm Duw?
Lle bu yn gyrchfan teuluoedd, trigolion, ffyddloniaid,
Erbyn hyn twristiaid, pererinion ac ymwelwyr ddaw drwy'r
    drws.

I ymweld a cheisio canfod yno
Y gorffennol, yr hanes, y naws
a chwilio am Dduw pan fod ei angen.
Ac mae yno o hyd, yn ofalgar, yn oddefgar yn gwrando,
yn arwain – os y clywn.

Pennant Melangell.

Y Santes a ochelodd ysgyfarnog fach dan ei chlogyn
rhag rhaib cŵn hela'r tywysog wrth iddi weddïo.
Y cŵn yn llonydd a methu symud wrth weld y forwynig
    mewn gweddi
a'r corn ynghlwm wrth wefusau'r heliwr hy.

Distawrwydd, tawelwch.

Clinc y drws wrth ymadael
a throi am adre gan feddwl am
ddoe,
heddiw,
fory,
trennydd,
a thradwy.

Beth a fu?
Beth sydd?
Beth a ddaw?

Teithio,
Troedio,
Tramwyo.

Gyda ffrind.

ALYSON EVANS

Light at St Davids

Light is an element
a medium, a portion
of clarity.

In darker seasons
it hums with a sheen of pewter
on flanks of a barn,

flaring thin fire
on grouted roofs and boundary stones,
walls scabrous with last year's whitewash.

It is a pearl, early wordless space,
brittle with newness, descending
a long toll of steps

to a stone lantern,
an emanation of rock and spume.
On the walls of the Bishop's Palace

sleepy jackdaws stutter into life,
their speech diffident, uncertain,
crumbly with dawn, as a mild syrup of light

pours into the stone frieze,
a child's paper fretwork, hinting
pink arabesques on the inner lip of a flower.

Glenda Beagan

42

St Beuno's Church, Llanycil

After the final footsteps came the silence,
deep as the lake itself, empty as space.
Inside the nave, a thin, grey haze of dust
settled on pew and font, on altar-rail
and cross; a dampness formed like drops of sweat
on brass, stone, iron, as the evening light,
peering through tear-stained images of glass,
cast a thin wash of colour on the walls.

And now the church turns in upon itself,
rewinds the spool of memory and replays
its past. Slowly at first, like visitors unsure
of where to sit, parishioners return
to their remembered places in the nave.

The oil lamps glow, the congregation stands
while hymns, psalms, sermons, prayers and litanies
re-echo from the consecrated walls.

Nothing is lost forever; like a shell
that keeps within its spiralled labyrinth
a memory of the ocean, this old place
still holds within its ancient prayer-drenched walls
echoes of worship; whisperings of faith,
half heard above the creaking of the pews,
the swallows in the eaves, the scampering
of nervous, unseen creatures in the aisles.

Outside, a bitter wind ruffles the lake,
a blast from Aran bends the wind-stressed yews,
scattering the churchyard birds like small black prayers.

DEREK THORP

43

A Hymn to St Dyfnog and his Well

(This hymn is sung in Llanrhaeadr-yng-Nghinmeirch on St Dyfnog's Day, 13 February.)

We praise the saints of every clime,
Today St Dyfnog is the prime,
To keep St David's bees decreed,
Producing honey and sweet mead.

But came the time when David turned
To water only – therefore spurned
The mead, and strong drink did forego
And Dyfnog found he had to go!

To sail to Ireland first he tried,
But, lo, the bees were at his side!
So sadly he was put ashore –
To Ireland went he nevermore.

So back to David Dyfnog hied,
'Go north, my son,' the saint replied,
And so St Dyfnog took his way
And sought a fitting place to stay.

He came upon a wooded dell,
And there a spring and ancient well.
So Dyfnog founded there his 'llan' –
To preach the gospel he began.

Long after Dyfnog's day, the well
Brought pilgrims to that wooded dell,
To try the healing waters' power
And in the church to pray an hour.

Like pilgrims old, in this our age,
Remember Dyfnog, faithful sage,
Remember in his church to pray
And serve our Saviour day by day.

HELEN JENKIN JONES

Cywydd i Ddyfnog

(This poem and useful references can be found in *Celtic Britain and the Pilgrim Movement* by G. Hartwell Jones.)

Dyfnog wr dwfn a garaf
am a dal f'oes mi ai dy-laf
dof ith eglwys ddwys yn Ddol
Llanrhaiadr mewn lle rheiol
dy ddelw di addolwn
dy liw yn wir dy lun a wnn
yn y nef ith gartrefwyd
da gida Duw geidwad wyd
dy wrthiau am diwarthawdd
yn y man hwnn ym yn hawdd
pistill o waith hapusteg
a roed it wr radau teg
mawr ei glod miragl ydyw
ffrwd groiwdeg or garreg yw
ffynnon or eigion a red
ragorawl i roi gwared
triagl heb swnd or grwndwal
ni wyr dyn yn aur a dal
Rhaiadr gras i bob nasiwn
er rhad a hap y rhoed hwnn
dwfr rhagorol feistriolaeth
presen ni wyr pris a wnaeth
prif afon seion sydd
berw llawn a bair llawenydd
arwydd enwog Jorddonen
gradd a ffons oi gwraidd ai phen

gwneuthur yn eglur a wna
uwch ei deml iechyd yma
golchi clwyf o gylch cleifion
a bwrw eu haint a bair honn
erioed gwneuthur yr ydoedd
y claf yn iach coelfaen oedd
Dyfnog hael da ofyn ced
breua gwr a bair gwared
attad y rhed y gwledydd
wrthyt sal o wrthiau sydd
pob cul afiach pob clefyd
pob gwann o bedwar bann byd
pob efrydd rhwymafrwydd rhus
pob nifer pob anafus
ebrwydd fydd yn rhydd ir rhain
mawredd oth wrthiau mirain
pob dall gweled ni allai
glod dy nerth gweled a wnai
pob byddar cynnar eu ced
yn glaiar gwnai i glywed
dy ras aml a droes yma
pob mud i ddwedyd yn dda
gwewyr oerion gair irad
ar frech wenwynig oer frad
ith bistill ced cyrched cant
gwych feddwl ag iach fyddant
oth fraint lle mynnaist oth fro
bennadur sant benydio
oerni y dwr arnad oedd
garw gadarn or garreg ydoedd

hynn a droes fawr einioes fri
einioes yn iechyd ini
tra fuost difost ofeg
urddwr dysg ar y ddaiar deg
rhodres byd nai wrhydri
mewn ystad nis mynnaist di
gwrthod yr holl bechodau
cordio'n fraisg caru Duw'n frau
gwisgo Crist a gwasgu'r croen
rhawn dewbais nid rhan diboen
a haiarn cadarn yn cau
fu ith gylch o faith gylchau
ni fynnaist nerth aberthwr
yn dy bryd ond bara a dwr
er ynnill gwlad y tad hen
berffaith heb drangc na gorffen.

NYS GWYDDUS PWY A'I CANT

Cywydd to Dyfnog

Dyfnog, sage, my devotion
and life's dues to thee I bring.
To thy hallowed church I come
in Llanrhaeadr's fine dale.
I thy image have adored,
and thy countenance I know.
Now is heaven thy home to dwell
with the Sun of Righteousness.
All thy mighty miracles
in this place do us restore.
A joyous fountain was to
thee vouchsafed, oh man of grace.
Wondrous miracle, we see
from the rock a crystal stream,
waters flowing to the well,
ever potent and relieving.
Soothing salve from earth does rise
beyond price in terms of gold,
cascade of grace for nations,
a gift of heavenly blessings,
its power all surpassing,
we can't know its worth to us.
Zion's river in full flow
surges forth with mighty joy.
Jordan's merit here is seen
in the spring-head, gloriously,
on display for all to see,

crowning its healing temple.
Here, sores of the sick are bathed,
and quenched are all their fevers.
Ever a source of healing:
a pillar bearing witness.
Dyfnog, to all supplicants
unfailing in thy bounty,
thee they seek from many lands
for miracles of healing.
All illness, all diseases,
all the weak, from all the earth,
all the world's maimed, hurt and bound,
all folk infirm and ailing,
will release and freedom find
by thy wondrous miracles.
All the blind who could not see
by thy power re-gained sight.
All the deaf who sought thy aid
re-gained hearing, crystal clear.
By thy abundant graces
all the dumb found eloquence.
Sufferers of torments sharp,
victims of the smallpox, all
to thy well in hundreds come
and are cured body and soul.
Merit from that sacred site,
where thou didst thy penance make
as the frigid waters flowed
from the rock to cleanse thy guilt,
has become, great soul, for us
a life-giving source of health.

While thou humbly didst impart
gifts of learning in our land,
worldly pomp and vanity
had no part to play for thee.
Never falling into sin,
love of God sustaining thee.
Though skin chafed, thou put on Christ,
sackcloth was thy raiment then,
held in place with iron hoop -
thee encircling, penance paid.
Strong abstainer, all thy needs
were by bread and water met.
Life in heaven with the Father
thou hast gained for evermore.

Poet unknown

TRANSLATION BY E. GWYNN MATTHEWS

Ffynnon Sant Dyfnog

Yn ôl yr hen, hen hanes
Am Ddyfnog, gwn un peth –
Âi lan i'r ffynnon yn y coed
Bob bore yn ddi-feth.

Ac yno, âi i mewn i'r dŵr
Hyd ei geseiliau – hyn bob tro,
Gweddïai'n daer am ffyniant
Y bobl yn y fro.

Fe euthum innau draw i'r fan
Un bore, fel 'rhen Sant,
A gwylio'r dŵr yn llifo'n chwim
O'r ffynnon draw i'r pant.

Ac yno, yn y fangre hud,
Gweddïais innau yn fy nhro
Y byddai Cymry heddiw'n driw
I Dduw, eu hiaith a'u bro.

HELEN JENKIN JONES

Nefyn to Aberdaron

When Bjorn Borg won again,
my winnings were ice cream
from the Post Office by the well.
As I stood at the kiosk, monks
tramped onwards, ignoring me.

When Liverpool lost the Cup,
I was in Aberdaron running up
and down the bridge, counting
pennies in Uncle Bob's Spar.
The saints were there, too, waiting.

When I sat on gorse and looked to Enlli
I could see houses, even stones
on boundary walls. See!
My thumb is bigger than an island!
But we can't go there.

The water is rough, deep and dark.
Pilgrims know the shortest journey
is the longest. And when home
feels strange and stark,
it's time to start walking.

MANON CERIDWEN JAMES

Taliesen continues his journey

I was the fox along the road
I was the man you did not see
Climbing down from the hill again
And the man you saw, that too was me
I was the shepherd, the sheep were mine
I was the sheep that went astray
I was the priest who broke the bread
I was the ploughman, turning the clay...
I was the worm in the soft red earth
I was the corpse that beneath it lay.

JOHN POOLMAN

Exile and Return

1

"Golden slumbers kiss your eyes,
smiles awake you when you rise.
Sleep, pretty darling, do not cry,
and I will sing a lullaby."

O the long sleep of childhood, such sweet dreams,
snatches of old songs, 'green and yellow'.
Summer days with sand beneath our feet,
between our toes warm sand of the dunes
and light, wind in our hair.
At night the song of the sea.

One day a turn, a breath of something
new, spring in the air.
The lane was full of celandines
and in the garden
I said, 'Mother, will I always be happy?'

*   *   *

Vivid dreams before waking,
how nearly real and how well remembered.

The heady air of Austria.
Reaching heights my own two feet had never reached before
I found blue gentians growing on the Gerlitzen.
In Sarajevo we discovered mosques and dark Eastern
    churches

and put our feet in the assassin's footprints.
Sleeping on trains through Italy, we reached Agrigento.
Among the temples one long moonlit night a Sicilian played
    the Jew's harp.

One summer then I cycled home from Wales.

*   *   *

I awoke
under a grey sky
and knew
I had left home.

'Make my bed quickly'

By the river's fallow waves
seabirds screamed.

'And I want to lie down'

Between tall houses
asphalt rang hard beneath my shoes.
I sought the forest
but they had strewn the paths with gravel.
I began to run.
In the growing darkness I ran on,
seeking the soft ground beneath the pines.
There I lay down,
pushing hands and face
into the cold earth.

"Once there was a way to get back homeward,
once there was a way to get back home.
Sleep, pretty darling, do not cry,
and I will sing a lullaby."

(Interlude)

A tamarisk hedge,
a five-barred gate,
slate stile.
Beyond: the sea.

I know where the wreck is,
and the spring in the rocks.

Once I imagined walking on the water,
there where the setting sun makes a golden path across the
    waves.

2

In the place by the sea
is a spring.
I know where it is –
and cannot find it.

I have travelled inland
seeking one I loved.
I am weary with travelling.
I have asked of friends, and strangers,
in places where I stayed, in lovers' arms –
they do not know where she is.

I am dried up.

Alone in the desert – since
there is nowhere else –
I hear the song of the sea.
Alone in the desert – since
there is no-one else –
I find my love.
She is dried up.
She is caked and crusted
with salt, of the years,
the tears of my searching.

Sing to her, sing gently. Do not break
the crust, or you will hurt her. But take
her gently, carry her all the way to the sea.
And hurry! the tide has ebbed
and is turning. And she is yearning
    to be free.

For I found the spring again
(I knew where it was – was it hidden?)
and I cupped my hand
and splashed my face, and drank,
and took off my shoes
and ran down the beach
and roared
with the roar of the sea.

SALLY ROGERS

Coracle

so we make shapes
with the crude instrument of our imaginings
snail-shell spiral
circumference of sun
arc of crescent moon
diameter of horizon
we take the willow
six months in the drying
& weave the basket of our dreamscape
such prosaic preparation
stitched with sinuous care
plump with promise
becomes
the hollow apricot of hope

PETER WALKER
(from *Old Men in Jeans*, 2012)

To Touch the Box

I journey partway by train
sharing a carriage
with commuters.
Then, for a short time,
a car with friends.
But the final mile
is on foot, and alone.

As I pass through the quiet
country town, stride down
the narrow pebbled lane,
the years disappear
as the miles have done,
and I walk in homespun,
wear a scallop shell
on my shoulder,
a satchel on my back,
carry a pilgrim's staff
to mark my steps.

Then I reach
the steel-studded door,
step across the threshold…
and all the years
between my selves,
sing there,
in the silence.

Slowly I cross the nave,
kneel to beg absolution,
then turn to the oaken casket
that is lit with candles,
framed by flowers.
I acknowledge the light,
the perfume, then lean between
the black iron bars,
to touch the box,
that holds the bones,
of a saint.

MAUREEN COPPACK

May Hill

Gusting wind: plain chant.

That sound carries me west of Severn,
to where the elm trees cease
and land rises to meet wide sweeping skies.

Here, where bright spring clouds scud
and larks sparkle the air with rising song,
we trod the rainsoft turf.

Our breath was gulped
from sky-streaming masses,
our steps made small by the arc of hill.

At the apex, by the ring of giants,
we halted for a wind-sung moment,
to lean against an ancient bole.

Looking up I glimpsed the arc of his back
against those raging branches,
his head defiant against a scudding sky

and on my hand, his caring grip.
That day, one of the first we had,
father and son alone.

Now gusting winds, which brought us to that moment
on the sacred hill, can bring me
to lean against a greater strength.

ANDREW SUMNER

Edington Priory Church

For centuries the canons chanted praise in you
Today you sail a proud ship still
Serene upon the chalk's calm ocean.

JOHN POOLMAN

The Pilgrims' Way

Pilgrims they are travellers
Who walk a special path,
The route is planned beforehand
The rest is left to faith.

The journey may be pleasant
Some days, though, may be rough,
But they carry on regardless
To journey is enough.

They may walk with companions
Or just meet along the way,
They'll take in all the sights and sounds
That come with each new day.

But what of those who cannot walk
Whose limits it would breach?
They too have a journey
A sacred place to reach.

Within four walls they may not
Smell the air nor feel the rain,
But the One who walks with pilgrims
Sits beside them just the same.

So let us pray for pilgrims
Where'er they walk or sit,
That all the paths they "travel"
With God's love may be lit.

ISOBEL JONES

By Another Way

It was the way back
and we were stepping into
our own shadows, for the western
sun was at our shoulder;
lighting our path with the light
of where we had been and seen
the extra-ordinary ordinary.
God, caught, at the mercy
of a myriad presumptions.

The road was new, yet not beyond
our knowing. Landmarks we had
passed and noted no longer found
a place on our map. The direction
was within and took us to a breaking.
A parting that proposed the path
for each of us to travel alone.

We had left behind our wisdom's
gifts and travelled wiser now and
lighter, as we made for home
in the East, where the narrowing
path led to the dawn of our
knowing as we had been known.

LLEWELYN ROGERS

Epilogue

for in the end
is our beginning

we are now soot-black silhouettes
against the crimson clouds

one last cormorant
wings stretched
posed like a crucifix
soaking up the fading embers of sunfire
before the tide reclaims his perch
& brings salty life to crusted barnacle & bladder-wrack

footsore, weary
emptied of pride & hungry for grace
we become a child again
open, trusting, waiting to be filled

for in the end
is our beginning

there is another path
another way
another day of learning what we can live without
another day of learning
when to give & when to hold
when to be still & when to run
when to prize fellowship & when solitude

to value all the little things we share

there is another path
another way
another day of learning what we must do without

for in the end
is our beginning

Peter Walker